Journey to Bethlehem

A nativity play

Sheila Lane and Marion Kemp

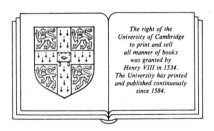

The right of the
University of Cambridge
to print and sell
all manner of books
was granted by
Henry VIII in 1534.
The University has printed
and published continuously
since 1584.

CAMBRIDGE   UNIVERSITY   PRESS

Cambridge

London   New York   New Rochelle

Melbourne   Sydney

Journey to Bethlehem

This story of the Nativity is taken from the New Testament. The information from the Bible has been filled out to make a play about the journey to Bethlehem by members of the family of the house of David, the shepherds and the wise men.

The journeys are linked by songs and carols, which can be sung by a choir or spoken by narrators.

Contents

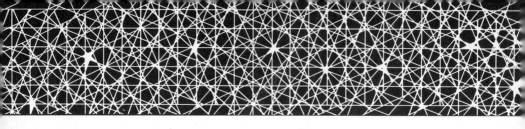

No room in the inn

(To be spoken or sung as an introduction.)

When Caesar Augustus had raised a taxation,
He assessed all the people that dwelt in the nation;
The Jews at that time being under Rome's sway
Appeared in the city their tribute to pay.

Then Joseph and Mary, who from David did spring,
Went up to the city of David their king,
And, there being entered, cold welcome they find –
From the rich to the poor they are mostly unkind.

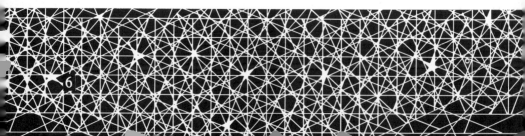

In the Town of Nazareth

Playmakers

ROMAN SOLDIER
JUDEAN SOLDIER

BRUTUS ⎤
CASCA ⎦   Roman messengers

SAMUEL ⎤
RACHEL ⎥   members of a family
NAOMI ⎥   of the house of Asher
JOSHUA ⎦

LEVI ⎤
NATHAN ⎦   members of a family of the house of Horab

JOSEPH ⎤
MARY ⎦   members of a family of the house of David

ZACHARIAS – a priest
ELIZABETH – his wife

Other people of the town

In the Town of Nazareth

The ROMAN *and* JUDEAN SOLDIERS *come into the empty market place and set up a Roman standard.*

ROMAN SOLDIER   Is this the place?

JUDEAN SOLDIER   Yes! This is Nazareth's market place.

ROMAN SOLDIER   Your villages and towns all look the same, Judean. They are so dry . . . and empty.

JUDEAN SOLDIER   Judea is not like Rome! What of it?

ROMAN SOLDIER   Ah! Rome is full of gaiety and life. The people talk and laugh and sing. Why won't you Judeans talk?

JUDEAN SOLDIER   We talk amongst ourselves, Roman.

ROMAN SOLDIER   Then why won't you talk with us?

JUDEAN SOLDIER   You Romans are overlords . . . we dare not talk.

ROMAN SOLDIER   It is not like that in other countries where we Romans rule. You Judeans are afraid. Is it your king who makes you fearful?

JUDEAN SOLDIER   (*fearfully*) Psst! Our king gives orders and we obey.

ROMAN SOLDIER   Herod! He is only King of Judea. He is only a . . . little king.

JUDEAN SOLDIER   Psst! The king . . . our king . . . is not little. He is . . .

ROMAN SOLDIER   What is he, Judean? Tell me about King Herod.

JUDEAN SOLDIER   Psst! (*looks round*) We do not even speak his name . . . we must not.

ROMAN SOLDIER   It is not like that with our emperor in Rome. Do you know, my friend, I have travelled in every part of the great Roman Empire, but there is no place on earth like Rome.

(*Enter* ROMAN MESSENGERS.)

BRUTUS You speak the truth, good soldier.

CASCA There is no place on earth like Rome.

BRUTUS (*pointing*) I see that the emperor's standard is set up. But where are the Nazarenes? We must put out Caesar's decree within the hour.

CASCA Do the people of the town know that we are here, Judean?

JUDEAN SOLDIER They do, my lords.

BRUTUS Then where are they?

JUDEAN SOLDIER King Herod's order was for all the Nazarenes to meet you here two hours before sun-down.

CASCA Which is about now. Why don't they come, Judean?

JUDEAN SOLDIER The Nazarenes were ordered to come to the market place two hours before sun-down. Not before that time, not after that time, but at that time.

BRUTUS (*scornfully*) Such obedience! He is not an emperor – this Herod of yours – just King of Judea.

CASCA It is not like this in Rome!

BRUTUS (*thoughtfully*) Caesar Augustus is above all kings and princes, but he is not feared as this Herod is.

CASCA I cannot understand it.

JUDEAN SOLDIER (*bitterly*) You would, my lords! You would . . . if . . .

ROMAN SOLDIER If what, my friend? You can speak freely to these Roman lords.

JUDEAN SOLDIER Nothing! I have said too much.

BRUTUS You have said nothing yet. (*enquiringly*) Does King Herod treat his subjects cruelly?

JUDEAN SOLDIER	(*shouts*) I know nothing! (*He moves away from the Romans.*)
CASCA	He is afraid. (*pointing*) But see! The Nazarenes! (*looking up at sun*) It is just on the hour, good Brutus.
	(*Groups of Nazarenes come in silently.*)
BRUTUS	Greetings to the people of Nazareth!
	(*All Nazarenes are silent.*)
	Well, how say you?
	(*All Nazarenes are silent*).
	(*loudly*) I bring greetings from great Caesar, Emperor of Rome.
	(*All Nazarenes are silent.*)
CASCA	It has been like this in all of Herod's lands – this silence.
BRUTUS	My friends, we do not come from Herod. Have no fear! We come from Rome. The emperor there rules over Herod. Caesar Augustus is the mightiest man on earth. So . . . how say you?
SAMUEL	We, the family of Asher, listen to your words, my lord.
CASCA	What about the rest of you?
LEVI	We, the family of Horab, listen.
JOSEPH	And we, the family of David, listen.
BRUTUS	(*shrugging shoulders*) As you will! Now, hear the decree of Caesar Augustus, Emperor of Rome.
	(*reads*) I, CAESAR AUGUSTUS, EMPEROR OF ROME, TO WHOM ALL KINGS, PRINCES AND PROVINCIAL GOVERNORS ARE SWORN TO GIVE ALLEGIANCE, AND TO WHOM I, CAESAR, GIVE PROTECTION, DO DECLARE THAT THERE SHALL BE A CENSUS OF ALL

PEOPLES. FOR THIS PURPOSE EVERY MAN AND WOMAN SHALL REGISTER IN THE CITY OF THEIR BIRTH AND SO THE POPULATION OF THE WHOLE EMPIRE SHALL BE COUNTED.

(looking at Nazarenes) Do you understand?

NAZARENES *(mutter)* Register . . . Register . . .

CASCA You must register before the month ends.

SAMUEL You give us very little time.

BRUTUS We have had many towns and villages to visit . . . but you have time. Make your preparations soon.

LEVI Must we go to the city of our birth?

JOSEPH We, the family of David, come from a distant place called Bethlehem.

CASCA Then you, of the family of David, must go to Bethlehem.

BRUTUS All those people who have been under the rule of Caesar must pay for the protection they have received from him.

NAZARENES PAY? PAY!

CASCA Yes! You must pay!

BRUTUS The registration has been decreed so that all people shall pay to Caesar that which is due to him – in taxes.

NAZARENES *(angrily)* Taxes! Taxes!

ROMAN SOLDIER The decree has been spoken and heard.

JUDEAN SOLDIER Shall we move on, my lord Brutus?

BRUTUS Let's away!

(BRUTUS, CASCA, ROMAN *and* JUDEAN SOLDIERS *go out.*)

SAMUEL A new taxation! So that is why we were called together.

11

RACHEL   We cannot pay more taxes.

NAOMI   What right has this Emperor of Rome to put more taxation on us?

JOSHUA   I have the answer! We won't register! How can these Romans find out about us if we don't register our family name? Tell me that.

LEVI   They'll soon find out about your family, Joshua. There are enough of you!

NATHAN   There are as many Ashers as there are birds of the air!

SAMUEL   It isn't so bad for you Horabs. You can all register nearby, but the family of Asher comes from across the River Jordan. It would take many days to walk back there.

LEVI   You are very silent, Joseph.

NATHAN   Where is it that you Davids have to go?

JOSEPH   To Bethlehem! But . . . my wife, is soon to have a child and it is so far to Bethlehem. The baby is due at this month's end. Mary cannot travel to Bethlehem now.

LEVI   It would be hard for her to go. Why don't you ask your friend Zacharias, the priest, what you should do?

NATHAN   Zacharias will know the law on this. Go and ask him what you should do about Mary.

JOSEPH   I will. I will do that. (*He goes out.*)

SAMUEL   There goes a good man.

RACHEL   Yes! Joseph the Carpenter is a good man. He is not like us in his ways.

NAOMI   There is something special about Joseph which makes him different. But, as you say, he is a good man.

12

JOSHUA	And he's clever with his hands! But come . . . it's time we Ashers used our heads. There must be something we can do about this taxation.
LEVI	(*to Joshua*) You heard the Roman! There is no way out.
NATHAN	You Ashers will have to obey the law in this and register your names.
SAMUEL	You are right, Nathan. There is no way out for any of us. The family of Asher must make preparations. Come!

(SAMUEL, RACHEL, NAOMI *and* JOSHUA *go out.*)

LEVI	We Horabs must do the same. This is a time for families to stay close together.
NATHAN	What about Joseph and Mary? I wonder . . . Ah! Here they come.

(JOSEPH *and* MARY *come in followed by* ELIZABETH *and* ZACHARIAS. MARY *sits down beside* JOSEPH.)

Good day to you all.

ZACHARIAS	Peace in the Lord!
NATHAN	What news in the temple today, Zacharias?
ZACHARIAS	The talk about new taxes is on those lips that should be speaking in soft prayers.
ELIZABETH	I fear that people will have less to give to the temple if they must pay more to Rome.
ZACHARIAS	We must pray to the Lord, Elizabeth.
ELIZABETH	What it is to have a husband who is a priest! Now we have a child in our old age, we must think of how we shall provide for him.
ZACHARIAS	The Lord will provide, wife. Trust in the Lord.
ELIZABETH	I do trust in the Lord, Zacharias. And I give thanks for my young John each day, but I have to feed him too.

LEVI	Life is hard for all of us. But what of Mary and this journey to Bethlehem? What's to be done, Joseph?
JOSEPH	I have prayed to God.
NATHAN	But what is the law on this, Zacharias? What is the law?
ZACHARIAS	There is nothing in the temple law about such things.
ELIZABETH	There should be! I say that Mary can stay with me and Joseph should go alone. He can explain when he registers in Bethlehem that Mary is soon to have a child and so she has not made the journey. I say . . .
ZACHARIAS	You say too much, wife.
ELIZABETH	And you say too little which is of any use, husband. You might just as well have stayed dumb. Don't forget that it was I who had our child christened by the Lord's chosen name. It is the women of the world who get things done.
ZACHARIAS	Peace woman! There is nothing in the temple law to help us in this. The decree is from Rome, not God.
ELIZABETH	But it is not possible for Mary to travel the long road to Bethlehem.
ZACHARIAS	With God all things are possible. God smiled on us, Elizabeth, in our old age and we were given our son, John. As I have said, with God all things are possible.
MARY	(*looking up*) That is what the angel said.
ALL	(*wonderingly*) Angel?
ZACHARIAS	You have not spoken of this before, Mary.

MARY	The angel of the Lord came to me and said, 'Fear not Mary, for thou hast found favour with God.'
ZACHARIAS	What else?
MARY	The angel said, 'The power of the Highest shall overshadow thee.' I am not afraid. I shall go to Bethlehem. God's power will care for me.

(JOSEPH *puts arm protectively round* MARY'S *shoulder as they go out.*)

| ZACHARIAS | (*wonderingly*) Blessed be the Lord God of Israel. The Lord shall give light to those that dwell in darkness. He shall guide all our feet in the way of peace. |

(ZACHARIAS, ELIZABETH, LEVI *and* NATHAN *go out, saying, 'Blessed be the Lord God of Israel.'*)

END OF FIRST PLAY

In the bleak mid-winter

In the bleak mid-winter
   Frosty wind made moan,
Earth stood hard as iron,
   Water like a stone;
Snow had fallen, snow on snow,
   Snow on snow,
In the bleak mid-winter,
   Long ago.

☆   ☆   ☆

Oh, who would be a shepherd boy?

Oh, who would be a shepherd boy,
And mind a flock of sheep,
While other men and boys enjoy
A quiet night of sleep?

Yes, who would choose to pass the night
In darkness and in cold?
Or hear the cry without a fright:
'The wolf is in the fold'?

The Shepherds

Playmakers

MALACHI AHAZ HEZRON	old shepherds

DAVID   a young shepherd who is lame

Other young shepherds

LABAN JESSE REUBEN ESAU	Laban's group of shepherds

ADAM BENJAMIN DANIEL JOEL	Adam's group of shepherds

Other shepherds from the hills

ASA SARA ZADOK REBEKAH	travellers, members of a family of the house of David

The Shepherds

The OLD SHEPHERDS *walk slowly into the shepherd's fold and huddle over the fire. Others, including the boy* DAVID, ADAM *and* BENJAMIN, *move about in the background.*

MALACHI There's snow on the hills tonight, brothers.

AHAZ Aye! And more to come! My old bones tell me that there's more to come.

HEZRON The shepherding will go hard tonight.

MALACHI Hard! Aye! It will be a hard night, but I wish that I could be out there on the hills, beneath the stars.

AHAZ You were always one for the hard work, Malachi. It was hard, but it was quiet up on the hills at this time of the year.

MALACHI Before the lambs came . . . before the births. It was always quiet before the births. There was always a kind of . . . peace. I remember it well.

(*The boy* DAVID *hobbles forward, listening.*)

AHAZ Remember! Aye! Remember! That's all we old ones can do.

HEZRON That's all that's left for the old ones. Just a place by the fire and remembering old times.

DAVID When I am old, I shall have no memories . . . no memories of winter nights on the hillside with the sheep . . . and wolves!

AHAZ Stay by the fire and be glad, boy.

DAVID I can't be glad. I would accept all the hardships if I could be out there.

HEZRON	Come to the fire, David. We will tell you tales of sheep . . . and wolves.
DAVID	(*bitterly to himself*) Tales! (*gently to old shepherds*) Tell me your tales, old men.
	(LABAN, JESSE, REUBEN *and* ESAU *come in, from the hills.*)
LABAN	Move over, old ones! Let us feel the fire. We're frozen to the marrow.
JESSE	It's a bitter night out there, grandfathers.
REUBEN	Let's have hot wine, to warm our bellies.
ESAU	Boy! David! Stir yourself!
DAVID	Am I always to be a shepherds' serving boy, but never a shepherd? (*He serves wine.*)
LABAN	(*to young shepherds*) You young ones over there! Go and tend the flocks we've brought down to the fold.
JESSE	Don't stand there idle! Look to the ewes.
	(YOUNG SHEPHERDS *go out grumbling.*)
MALACHI	My legs are weak, but I'm still a shepherd. I know what should be done out there.
HEZRON	And I. We'll help with the ewes.
	(MALACHI *and* HEZRON *go out.*)
REUBEN	(*to* AHAZ) So you're staying by the fire, Ahaz. You're not going to see that the young ones do their work?
AHAZ	The young ones do not like old shepherds on their heels. They like to do the work without us.
ESAU	Like! Like! Who cares what the young ones like? Times have changed since I was a boy.

LABAN	Times haven't changed, Esau! Young ones always kick against old ones and their ways. I know I did!
ADAM	Come, Benjamin! It's time we took our turn out on the hills. Let's fill our bellies first.
BENJAMIN	Aye! It will be bitter cold out there.
JESSE	The white-faced sheep are all down here in the fold. The black-faced ones are out in the foothills.
REUBEN	It was strange out there tonight, Adam. Strange, as well as cold.
ESAU	The flocks were restless and uneasy.
ADAM	Then we'll be on our way to join the others.
BENJAMIN	Keep a good fire!
	(ADAM *and* BENJAMIN *go out.*)
ALL	Fare you well!
LABAN	Come! Let's settle by the fire. Aye! It was strange about the sheep tonight. I've never known ewes to be so nervous and uneasy at this time of year.
JESSE	And there were so many travellers about.
REUBEN	I've never seen so many people on the road, and at nightfall too. They must still be going to Bethlehem for the counting.
DAVID	If families of the house of David are still travelling to Bethlehem to be registered, there is time.
LABAN	What do you mean, boy?
DAVID	There is still time for me to go.
JESSE	You were excused . . .
DAVID	(*loudly*) But I should go. I am of the house and family of David. My name is David.

20

REUBEN	(*kindly*) No, lad! You cannot go.
DAVID	But there is time! (*quietly*) There is time!
ESAU	What's the matter with you boy? Are you weak in the head as well as in the legs? Do you think that someone will carry you to Bethlemen?
DAVID	(*bowing head*) No, I do not think that. But I think I should have tried to go. I have my crutch . . . I could have tried . . . I wanted to.

(MALACHI *and* HEZRON *come in, with travellers,* ASA, SARA, ZADOK *and* REBEKAH. *They are followed by the* YOUNG SHEPHERDS.)

MALACHI	Come travellers! Come into the fold. You are welcome here.
ASA	We give thanks, old man.
HEZRON	Make a place by the fire for these young people, shepherds. They are faint with cold and hunger.
ALL SHEPHERDS	Come in! Come in!
AHAZ	David! Bring wine for these travellers.

(DAVID *serves wine.*)

ALL TRAVELLERS	Our thanks to you all.
LABAN	Stretch out your limbs. The fire will comfort you. When we came off the hills, some little time ago, we were all numb with cold.
ASA	Your fire brings comfort to our bodies, but most we thank you for your welcome. It is the welcome that warms our hearts.
JESSE	What brings you here at this time of night, young friends?
ASA	We are travelling from the village where we live, for the counting, to be registered, as Caesar decreed.

REUBEN	(*laughing*) Good people! You cannot register with us!
ESAU	We are simple shepherds. We just count sheep!
	(*All laugh.*)
LABAN	You have wandered some distance from the highway. It is not wise to do that, you know.
SARA	We saw your light.
ZADOK	It drew us to the fold.
REBEKAH	And then we saw shepherds tending their sheep. Now you have tended us.
LABAN	You are welcome to what we have. But tell me, young people, to which city are you going?
ALL TRAVELLERS	To Bethlehem!
DAVID	Bethlehem! Then you are of the family of David. You are of my family. I am a David.
ASA	Greetings, brother David! We are from Zar, a small place beyond Nazareth.
DAVID	(*putting out arms*) Greetings, to all my family!
ASA	Greetings! We are late in making our journey, but if we set off early tomorrow, there will be time.
DAVID	Yes, there is still time.
SARA	Have you made the journey to Bethlehem, brother?
DAVID	No! Not me!
ZADOK	Not you?
REBEKAH	But you have just said that you are a David. All Davids must go to Bethlehem.
DAVID	(*turning away*) Not this one.
ASA	I don't understand.

LABAN   (*quietly*) This David was excused. Look at his legs and feet. This David . . . this brother of yours . . . is a cripple.

ASA   For my part, I did not see . . . his feet. (*turning to David*) David! Is it in your heart to go to Bethlehem?

DAVID   Aye! That it is. But the people here persuaded me to stay at home. They told me that I must stay.

SARA   The shepherds here are kindly people.

DAVID   Yes, they are good and kind. I know that.

ZADOK   Perhaps they are too kind, brother David.

DAVID   What do you mean? How can they be too kind?

REBEKAH   They are kind . . . and they care for you. But perhaps you should help yourself.

DAVID   (*surprised*) Help myself?

ASA   You are not helpless, David. You cannot expect to be carried to Bethlehem.

DAVID   That is what Esau said. Just before you came, he said, 'Do you think that someone will carry you to Bethlehem?'

ASA   And now we say the same. Bethlehem cannot be more than one day's walk from here.

DAVID   But I cannot walk. At least, I cannot walk as you do.

ASA   Then do it in the way you can. It may take two days, three or even four. But do it.

DAVID   People have not spoken to me in this way before.

SARA   Why don't you try?

DAVID   Will you help me to the highway, tomorrow, when you go?

ZADOK   We can do that.

REBEKAH	We'll do it willingly. We'll set you on your way.
ASA	BUT . . . we will not carry you.
DAVID	(*moving away*) Tonight . . . now . . . I will prepare myself. I'll fill my shepherd's bag with food and wine.
ASA	(*calls*) Enough for several days, David.
DAVID	Aye! When morning comes, I shall be ready. (*He goes out.*)
LABAN	Good young people, your kindness does you great credit. But this may not be wise . . .

(ADAM, BENJAMIN, JOEL, DANIEL *and other* SHEPHERDS *from the hillside, enter in great haste.* DAVID *follows on his crutch.*)

ADAM	Brothers! Brothers! We've brought . . . tidings!
BENJAMIN	TIDINGS OF GREAT JOY!
ADAM	We have seen . . . ANGELS!
ALL LISTENERS	Angels! (*unbelievingly*) ANGELS!
LABAN	Where?
JOEL	Out there! On the hillside!
DANIEL	In the sky!
JESSE	(*in amazement*) Out there on the hillside? In the sky?
REUBEN	The cold has turned their heads.
ESAU	Aye! It is a bitter night. Come, Reuben! We must go to the sheep. There is no-one to keep watch.

(ESAU *and* REUBEN *go out.*)

ADAM	Listen! It was like this . . . We were, as you know, on the foothills with the black-faced sheep, keeping watch over the flocks, as we always do.
ALL LISTENERS	Aye! Aye!

BENJAMIN	It was Joel who saw it first. Tell what you saw, Joel.
JOEL	I turned my eyes up to the hills and there came . . . this great light. It was far off to begin with, but then it grew closer, scattering the darkness.
ALL LISTENERS	And then?
JOEL	I called to the others. I said, 'What has happened to the night?' I said that because it was night and yet is was as light as day.
ADAM'S SHEPHERDS	As light as day!
DANIEL	We all looked and we could see it too. It was above the hills. It seemed to be in the sky, and yet it was more than that . . . It was all around.
ADAM	We could all see it . . .
BENJAMIN	. . . and feel it around us.
MALACHI	(*puzzled*) We have all SEEN a light, but how could you FEEL it, brothers?
AHAZ	Did you feel it as we feel a fire?
HEZRON	Was it hot, like a fire?
	(ADAM'S SHEPHERDS *shake their heads.*)
MALACHI	Go on, brothers. Tell us more about the light you felt around you.
JOEL	(*excitedly*) The light was not on the hills, or in the sky . . . It was IN THE AIR. (*with excited gestures*) That's where it was.
MALACHI	(*patiently*) So . . . the light was 'in the air'. Now what of these ANGELS? Maybe it was the brightness of the light around you that made you think you saw some angels.
ADAM'S SHEPHERDS	No! No!
ADAM	They were real angels.
BENJAMIN	They spoke to us.

MALACHI	So . . . The angels spoke to you. What did they say?
JOEL	They brought news of a birth.
MALACHI	(*to listening shepherds*) So early, brothers! We were not expecting any lambs tonight . . . but it can happen. Births can be early.
DANIEL	The angels brought us tidings . . .
JOEL	. . . tidings of great joy . . . for ALL people.
ADAM	Then the angels spoke of a new birth.
MALACHI	Lambs are born all the time. There is nothing extraordinary about a lamb being born.
BENJAMIN	It is not a lamb we speak of!
JOEL	We are not talking about sheep and lambs.
DANIEL	This is a human birth!
MALACHI	A human birth, you say. (*He shrugs his shoulders.*) Well, human births happen all the time too.
AHAZ	There is nothing extraordinary in that.
HEZRON	It happens all the time. There's nothing extraordinary about a human birth.
MALACHI	Except to the parents, perhaps! So . . . there is a new baby somewhere tonight. There will be many more, brothers. There will be many births tonight, throughout the world.
ADAM	But not like this one. Tonight we saw the angel of the Lord God.
BENJAMIN	Don't you understand? The angel of the Lord came as we lay there on the hillside.
JOEL	The angel was there before us. It was the angel of the Lord who told us of a birth, over in David's town, which we call Bethlehem. A child has been born there. This is the birth we have been speaking of.

DANIEL	It may sound ordinary now, as we sit round the fire. But the extraordinary part is . . .
ADAM	The baby is to be a SAVIOUR!
ALL LISTENERS	A SAVIOUR!
BENJAMIN	He will be CHRIST THE LORD, a KING, for all mankind.
ALL LISTENERS	A KING!
JOEL	And most extraordinary of all . . . He has been born to poor parents, in a poor stable.
DANIEL	And his cradle will be a manger.
ADAM	So now you understand why we left the sheep.
BENJAMIN	Now you know why we came in such haste.
JOEL	You missed the angel's message, but you can share in the news. It is for all mankind, but especially for shepherds.
ALL LISTENERS	For us?
MALACHI	Why us? Why especially for shepherds?
DANIEL	It is as the prophets of old foretold.
ADAM	It is told in the prophet's Great Book. Don't you remember about the people who walked in darkness?
BENJAMIN	Yes! It said that they would see a great light. The people who walked in darkness are the shepherds on the hills at night.
ALL LISTENERS	(*doubtfully*) Maybe! Perhaps!
JOEL	I remember some more . . . It says, 'He shall feed his flock like a shepherd.' There! It says, 'like a shepherd'. It must be especially for shepherds.
DANIEL	It IS for shepherds and for all mankind. So come with us, now, to Bethlehem to see the child.
LABAN	Now? But the flocks are out on the hillside.

JESSE	Reuben and Esau are with them. The sheep will be quite safe.
LABAN	But can we be sure that this birth is so important? We went to Bethlehem some days ago, for the counting. We heard nothing of this then.
MALACHI	It had not happened then.
AHAZ	What do you mean, Malachi?
HEZRON	You sound as if you believe it, Malachi. Do you believe that something extraordinary has happened tonight, in Bethlehem?
MALACHI	Yes, I believe it has.
AHAZ	Shall we go to find this new-born child?
HEZRON	It is a long way for old bones, on such a night.
MALACHI	This is a new beginning. We shall not feel our years. Come, brothers!
AHAZ	You are father of us all in age, Malachi.
HEZRON	If you go, we shall follow.
	(*The three* OLD SHEPHERDS *go out.*)
LABAN	And we shall follow after. Come Jesse! We'll pen all the sheep down here in the fold, and follow after.
JESSE	We must all go, Laban. It is for all mankind, but especially for shepherds.
	(*All* SHEPHERDS *go out except David.*)
ASA	It is extraordinary that all this should have happened tonight, in David's town!
SARA	When we are on our way there.
ZADOK	We shall see the child. He will be a David.
REBEKAH	The Lord God has smiled on those misfortunes which made us late for the counting. Come, let's make our way with haste. (*She moves towards exit.*)

DAVID   Wait! You promised you would help me to the highway.

ASA   It is your time too, David. (*He smiles.*) It seems that you were not meant to go to Bethlehem before tonight.

DAVID   Now is my time! At last! I am going to Bethlehem.

(*All go out,* ZADOK *and* ASA *helping* DAVID.)

END OF SECOND PLAY

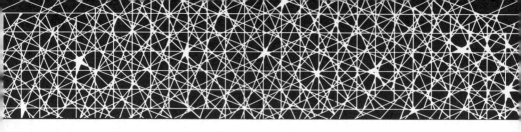

Three kings are here

Three kings are here, both wealthy and wise,
Come riding far over the snow-covered ice;
Royal in throng,
Noble in song,
They search for the child, the Redeemer of wrong;
With tambours and drums they go sounding along.

Kings of Orient

We three kings of Orient are;
Bearing gifts we traverse afar,
Field and fountain, moor and mountain,
Following yonder star;

O star of wonder, star of night,
Star with royal beauty bright,
Westward leading, still proceeding,
Guide us to thy perfect light.

A Village near Bethlehem

Playmakers

KING MELCHIOR
SHALIMAR his servant
PAGE
TWO CAMEL MEN

KING GASPAR
REZA his servant
PAGE
TWO BAGGAGE MEN

KING BALTHASAR
AMAT his servant
PAGE
TWO TENT BEARERS

OLD MAN ⎤
ANNA ⎟
RUTH ⎬ travellers, a family of the house of David
SIMON ⎟
JACOB ⎦

OBED ⎤
AZOR ⎦ Judean soldiers

Other soldiers

A Village near Bethlehem

It is late afternoon, and Melchior's servant, SHALIMAR, *is hurrying along a country road towards a village.*

SHALIMAR There must be an inn somewhere in the next village. (*He pauses.*) Ah! There is a light. May good fortune be with me. (*He begins to move on.*)

(*Enter* REZA *from left.*)

REZA Wait! Wait!

SHALIMAR Who goes there? Is it a friend?

REZA I come in friendship. Greetings!

SHALIMAR Greetings! Can you direct me to an inn? I am looking for a resting-place.

REZA Why, so am I! And so are all of us. (*He points down the road.*)

SHALIMAR Us! (*He draws back.*) I can only see one of you. Who is hiding in the shadows?

REZA (*holding out his hand*) Peace, friend! I am alone here. My master and his other servants are some way back. I called out because I need your help.

SHALIMAR My help! You will get no help from me if you are searching for an inn. Indeed, if there are many of you, I must hurry on.

REZA Wait! Let us search together. It is not yet dark. What is the haste?

SHALIMAR My master is a great and noble king. I have to find a resting-place for him and all his retinue. If there are others on the road it will be more difficult.

REZA A king you say?

SHALIMAR	(*with a superior smile*) A king . . . King Melchior!
REZA	(*holding out his hand*) So is my master! My master is a king.
SHALIMAR	Two kings here, in this miserable place! It is too strange to be true. No! This is some trick!
REZA	I give you my word. My master is a king. It is strange, but it is true. We have come far.
SHALIMAR	(*haughtily*) Indeed! You may serve a kind of king . . . from some little country . . . from some island throne, perhaps.
REZA	(*indignantly*) My master is a king. He is called Gaspar.
SHALIMAR	Just so! But I cannot stay here and talk. I must hurry on. If the people in the next village know that there are two kings seeking accommodation, they will put the prices up.
REZA	Hold! A stranger comes.

(AMAT *enters from the right.*)

SHALIMAR	Who goes there? Is it a friend?
AMAT	Peace brothers! I come in friendship. Greetings!
SHALIMAR	Greetings! (*to Reza*) Perhaps this is some fellow from the neighbourhood. (*moving towards Amat*) Now, tell me, fellow . . . where can I find rooms in a high class inn for my master and his retinue?
AMAT	(*in a disgruntled tone*) Don't ask me!
SHALIMAR	But I do ask you, fellow, so give me an answer. My master is a king and he requires rooms for the night. Mark you, the service must be good and the rooms must be clean. And there must be some place for the camels and the baggage men.
AMAT	(*bitterly*) Don't ask me! Don't talk to me about inns and rooms and resting-places. I must know

33

	more about dirty inns, bad-tempered landlords and lame camels than any man alive. And my master always blames me, of course!
REZA	We are looking for resting-places for the night too. Tell me . . . Who is your master?
AMAT	My master is a king.
SHALIMAR, REZA	(*looking at each other in astonishment*) A king!
SHALIMAR	It is not possible. Three kings here in this miserable place! It cannot be so.
AMAT	For my sins . . . I serve a king. His name is Balthasar.
REZA	(*with a quiet smile*) From some little country! My master is a king too. Tell us why your king comes here.
AMAT	You won't believe me if I do.
REZA	Go on!
AMAT	This king of mine, Balthasar, is a gloomy fellow. He reads a lot . . . and thinks . . . and stares at the sky. No matter, that is his way. But, some time ago, he saw a certain star!
SHALIMAR	(*in astonishment*) A star, you say! That is most strange. My master, King Melchior, is an astrologer.
REZA	Mine too! We are following a star.
AMAT	(*looking interested*) But where to? What is your destination?
REZA	Oh, we don't really know! My king, whose name is Gaspar, is a man with a happy heart. He says that in time . . . in time . . . we shall reach a place where there is another . . . greater king.
SHALIMAR	He must mean my master Melchior! Melchior is the greatest and most noble king in all the world.

It's clear to me now! Your kings have come to meet my Melchior.

REZA (*doubtfully*) Do you think that this (*pointing to the ground*) is the meeting place of kings?

AMAT My master says that when the new king is found, he will be living in poverty.

REZA (*smiling*) Then it cannot be your Melchior, my friend!

AMAT You won't believe this . . . but I'll tell you both . . . My master Balthasar believes that this new king is . . . a child.

SHALIMAR, REZA A child!

AMAT Just so! Balthasar had dreams . . . and ever since he has been restless. He cannot stay among his riches.

REZA Does he search and search and search?

SHALIMAR Looking for something which . . . he cannot name, perhaps?

AMAT (*nodding*) He does!

SHALIMAR And so does Melchior!

REZA My Gaspar is like this!

ALL THREE (*wonderingly*) God be with us!

(*Enter* MELCHIOR'S PAGE, *from centre back.*)

MELCHIOR'S PAGE Shalimar! Have you found a resting-place? King Melchior comes!

(*Enter* GASPAR'S PAGE, *from left.*)

GASPAR'S PAGE Reza! What news! King Gaspar comes!

(*Enter* BALTHASAR'S PAGE, *from right.*)

BALTHASAR'S PAGE Amat! King Balthasar is here!

(*Enter the three* KINGS *with* CAMEL MEN, BAGGAGE MEN *and* TENT BEARERS, *all singing.*)

35

ALL	We three kings of Orient are, Bearing gifts we traverse afar, Field and fountain, moor and mountain, Following yonder star.

(*They take up positions, with the Kings in the centre.*)

MELCHIOR	And so we three kings meet together.
GASPAR	Having followed the star from the East.
BALTHASAR	As it was written.
MELCHIOR	It has been a long and bitter journey.
GASPAR	Just the worst time of the year for such a journey.
BALTHASAR	But that is how it was written.
MELCHIOR	We must go on.
GASPAR	We must follow the star.
BALTHASAR	It is written that we must never give up.
ALL KINGS	We must go on.
ALL SERVANTS	Where do we go? Tell us where.
ALL KINGS	(*pointing the same way*) Following yonder star.

(*All except two camel men, two baggage men and two tent bearers, move off in procession, singing.*)

ALL	O star of wonder, star of night, Star with royal beauty bright, Westward leading, still proceeding, Guide us to thy perfect light.
FIRST CAMEL MAN	(*angrily*) We must follow the star, they say! We must never give up! We must go on! I served Melchior once, but I'm not going on!
SECOND CAMEL MAN	Nor I! I give up now!

36

FIRST BAGGAGE MAN	I served King Gaspar once, but not now!
SECOND BAGGAGE MAN	I'm not going on.
FIRST TENT BEARER	Good Balthasar was my king.
SECOND TENT BEARER	And mine till now.
FIRST CAMEL MAN	So we are of the same mind?
ALL SERVANTS	We are!
FIRST CAMEL MAN	We'll make this ground our resting place till morning. Let's sleep.
ALL SERVANTS	Let's sleep! (*They prepare for sleep, rolling themselves in their cloaks, grumbling and murmuring.*)
FIRST CAMEL MAN	(*sitting up*) I can hear voices!
ALL SERVANTS	(*in disgust*) Voices!
FIRST BAGGAGE MAN	Our kings heard voices! Let's hear no more of voices!
ALL SERVANTS	Let's sleep.
FIRST TENT BEARER	(*getting up*) Listen! There are travellers coming down the road towards this place.
	(*All sit up. Soft singing is heard in the distance.* SERVANTS *move aside. The* TRAVELLERS *come in softly singing, 'Kum Ba Yah'. They sit down.*)
RUTH	How far is it to Bethlehem?
OLD MAN	Not very far! If my memory serves me well, it is only a few hours' walk from the next village. It must be nearly three score years since I walked along this road.

ANNA	Did you go to Bethlehem to register the family all those years ago?
OLD MAN	Why, no! This is the first registration of its kind throughout the Roman world.
ANNA	Then why did you go?
OLD MAN	It was to bring your grandmother from our family city. Ah! The road seemed easier then.
SIMON	(*impatiently*) Come! We must be on our way.
JACOB	We have rested here too long already. It is getting dark.
OLD MAN	I know that. But these old bones of mine cry out for rest. I have a little money. Go to the next village, boys, and see if you can find rooms for the night.

(SIMON *and* JACOB *go out.* SERVANTS *move to centre.*)

FIRST CAMEL MAN	I wish them luck, old man.
OLD MAN	(*fearfully*) Who are you? What do you want of us? I have only one small loaf and a few figs.
FIRST BAGGAGE MAN	Have no fear! We are weary travellers like yourselves.
FIRST TENT BEARER	In God's name, we are too tired to harm you.
OLD MAN	Strong, grown men . . . too tired! Then why do you stay here? Are there no rooms in the village for travellers?
SECOND CAMEL MAN	They'll be taken now.
SECOND BAGGAGE MAN	Our kings will have the rooms if there are any to be had.

RUTH	Kings, you say? Who are your kings?
SECOND TENT BEARER	We are . . . We were, the servants of three great kings who have come from the East.
ANNA	(*in relief*) You don't serve . . . (*whispering*) Herod, then?
OLD MAN	So you have come from far-off lands?
FIRST CAMEL MAN	Indeed we have.
ALL SERVANTS	But now we go no farther. No!
OLD MAN	So you have forsaken your kings. (*wonderingly*) You have given up? Tell me! Do you intend to stay in this poor place for ever? Do you intend to end your days . . . here?
ALL SERVANTS	(*looking at each other*) We don't know. We hadn't thought . . .
FIRST BAGGAGE MAN	Where do you go old man?
FIRST TENT BEARER	And why?
OLD MAN	We are of the house . . . the family . . . of David. We are journeying to Bethlehem, which is our family city, in obedience to the emperor's decree. If we disobey the emperor's command, the king of this country (*whispering*) . . . King Herod . . . will punish us.
RUTH	No-one disobeys the king.
ANNA	Besides we want to register the family.
OLD MAN	Listen, my friends! This king of ours is without mercy, so do not offend the law while you are travelling through our country. If you do, you may end your days here after all, and sooner than you think!

FIRST CAMEL MAN	Your Herod cannot harm us.
FIRST BAGGAGE MAN	We have our own kings.
FIRST TENT BEARER	Melchior . . . Gaspar . . . and good Balthasar!
OLD MAN	No! They WERE your kings. You have forsaken them and given up your duty.
ALL SERVANTS	(*looking at each other*) We told you . . . We were tired . . . We hadn't thought . . .
OLD MAN	(*rather scornfully*) You're grown men and you've given up! Listen to my counsel! This king of ours has his spies abroad. He is uneasy! He has seen it in the stars that other kings will come this way and rival him. Take care, my friends!

(*Enter* SIMON *and* JACOB.)

RUTH	(*eagerly*) Did you find rooms?
ANNA	Did you find a place for us to rest till daybreak?
SIMON	(*despairingly*) There was nothing.
JACOB	We went to every house.
OLD MAN	Did you try the inn? The prices will be high, but I have a little money.
SIMON	We tried the inn.
JACOB	But there was no room.
OLD MAN	No room at the inn?
SIMON	No! There are so many travellers along this road.
JACOB	All going to Bethlehem like us.
OLD MAN	(*getting up slowly*) Then we must go on.
RUTH	(*looking into the distance*) Does the road wind up hill all the way?
OLD MAN	(*thoughtfully*) Aye! To the very end. The road is long and hard, but we must not give up. Never! Come!

	(*The* FAMILY GROUP *goes out.*)
FIRST CAMEL MAN	Perhaps they are right. (*looking round*) We can't stay here! Let's follow them to Bethlehem.
ALL	To Bethlehem!
	(*They begin to move off as* OBED, AZOR *and other Judean* SOLDIERS *come in.*)
OBED	Stand!
FIRST CAMEL MAN	Soldiers!
AZOR	Do not move! You are surrounded!
FIRST CAMEL MAN	Whose soldiers are you? Whom do you serve?
OBED	We serve King Herod.
ALL SOLDIERS	Herod, the strong! Herod the mighty! Herod, King of all Judea! HEROD! (*They raise their spears.*)
FIRST CAMEL MAN	So you do not speak King Herod's name in whispers!
	(SERVANTS *move forward cheerfully.*)
OBED	Stand!
AZOR	Fools! You heard our order! Stand! Keep well apart and do not move.
FIRST CAMEL MAN	Why do you treat us like this? We are friendly travellers and . . .
OBED	(*interrupting*) You are spies!
ALL SERVANTS	Spies! No! No!
AZOR	Then why are you here, moving about at night, after the curfew?
OBED	You! (*pointing to First Camel Man*) You with the tongue! Speak!
FIRST CAMEL MAN	What do you mean? (*in amazement*) We all have tongues.

OBED	But not for long! Wait till Herod hears of this.
AZAR	Why are you disobeying Herod's law? No-one may move about after the curfew, except on the highway. Why are you here?
FIRST CAMEL MAN	We are searching for our kings.
ALL SOLDIERS	(*in horror*) KINGS!
OBED	There is only one king.
ALL SOLDIERS	Herod, the strong! Herod, the mighty! Herod, King of all Judea! HEROD! (*They raise their spears.*)
FIRST CAMEL MAN	Listen! We are servants of three great kings who have come from the East.
OBED	Spies! They are spies from the East!
ALL SOLDIERS	SPIES!
AZOR	So you are the servants of three great kings who have come from the East?
ALL SERVANTS	Yes!
AZOR	And these three kings are here, in Judea?
ALL SERVANTS	Yes!
AZOR	Where are they, now?
FIRST CAMEL MAN	We don't know . . .
AZOR	(*angrily*) Don't know! Herod has ways of making people remember! (*He beckons to the soldiers.*) Tie them up! King Herod shall hear of this.
OBED	Can there be kings from the East travelling in Herod's land?
AZOR	And without his knowledge? It does not sound possible. We'll take these foreign servants to Herod's palace.

OBED We have done well for the king tonight, Azor.

AZOR (*to soldiers*) Take them away!

(SOLDIERS *and* SERVANTS *go out.*)

(*to Obed*) Yes! We have done well, Obed. But Herod is uneasy. It is said that he has seen it in the stars that other kings will come this way and rival him. King Herod does not like to hear of . . . other kings!

(OBED *and* AZOR *go out muttering,* 'Other kings . . . Other kings . . .')

END OF THIRD PLAY

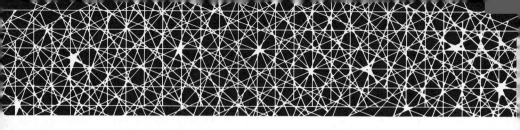

Song of the Nativity

1 How far is it to Bethlehem?
    Not very far.
Shall we find the stable-room
    Lit by a star?

2 Can we see the little child,
    Is he within?
If we lift the wooden latch
    May we go in?

3 May we stroke the creatures there,
    Ox, ass, or sheep?
May we peep like them and see
    Jesus asleep?

4 If we touch his tiny hand
    Will he awake?
Will he know we've come so far
    Just for his sake?

5 God in his mother's arms,
    Babes in the byre,
Sleep, as they sleep who find
    Their heart's desire.

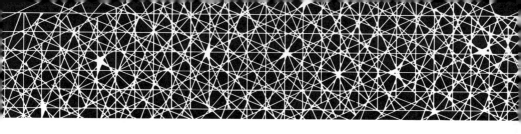

Standing in the rain

1 No use knocking on the window,
There is nothing we can do, sir.
All the beds are booked already –
There is nothing left for you, sir.

Chorus
Standing in the rain,
Knocking on the window,
Knocking on the window
On a Christmas Day.
There he is again,
Knocking on the window,
Knocking on the window
In the same old way.

2 Wishing you a merry Christmas,
We will now go back to bed, sir!
Till you woke us with your knocking
We were sleeping like the dead, sir.

In Bethlehem

Playmakers

INNKEEPER
INNKEEPER'S WIFE

From the first play
MARY

JOSEPH

From the second play
MALACHI

AHAZ

HEZRON

DAVID
Other young shepherds

ADAM

BENJAMIN

DANIEL

JOEL

LABAN

JESSE

REUBEN

ESAU
Other shepherds

ASA

SARA

ZADOK

REBEKAH

From the third play
KING MELCHIOR

SHALIMAR

PAGE

CAMEL MEN

KING GASPAR

REZA

PAGE

BAGGAGE MEN

KING BALTHASAR

AMAT

PAGE

TENT BEARERS

OLD MAN

ANNA

RUTH

SIMON

JACOB

In Bethlehem

SIMON *and* JACOB *hurry into the empty market place.*

SIMON   (*breathlessly*) Look brother! (*pointing*) There is a faint light! Perhaps it is a resting-place for travellers.

JACOB   If there are rooms, we must try to get them first.

SIMON   Can that poor place be Bethlehem's inn?

JACOB   Can this poor place be Bethlehem?

SIMON   Isn't it strange, brother? There were so many people on the road. But now we've arrived, we find the town is empty.

JACOB   It seems that we ran ahead for nothing. I suppose . . . this is Bethlehem?

SIMON   Where else can it be? Grandfather could not be mistaken. He has been before.

JACOB   I thought there would be so many travellers here, all come for the counting.

SIMON   Perhaps they are here, but in their beds! Look! There's the light again. It's moving.

JACOB   That means that there is someone about. Let's go and see.

SIMON   Our family is tired. We must find a comfortable resting-place for grandfather.

JACOB   Listen!

(*'Kum Ba Yah' is sung softly in the distance.*)

SIMON   That's our family. I'd know their voices anywhere.

(*The singing gets nearer.*)

JACOB	Can they have caught up with us so soon?

(*Enter* OLD MAN, RUTH *and* ANNA.)

RUTH	(*eagerly*) Have you found rooms for us, brother?
SIMON	We're not even sure if we've found Bethlehem!
JACOB	Is this Bethlehem, grandfather?
OLD MAN	This is Bethlehem, my children. (*He looks round.*) Ah! I remember it well. This is the place.
ANNA	At last! Bethlehem! Now where are we to stay? Have you found rooms, brothers?
SIMON	Not yet, but we've seen lights moving over there (*pointing*).
JACOB	(*excitedly*) Look! There are some more now. It must be an inn of some kind.
RUTH	Hurry brothers! There are many more travellers on the road.

(SIMON *and* JACOB *go out.*)

ANNA	And some are coming now.

(*Voices are heard off-stage.*)

OLD MAN	They will be Davids. Ah! It does my old heart good to be surrounded by my kinsmen.

(*Enter* ASA, SARA, ZADOK *and* REBEKAH.)

Greetings to you all! Greetings to all Davids!

ASA	Greetings to you all!

(*The groups exchange handshakes and greetings.*)

(*excitedly*) What have you found?

OLD MAN	Found? We have found Bethlehem!
ASA	But . . . what else?
RUTH	If you mean, 'Have we found rooms?' – we are not sure yet. Our brothers have gone to ask.

ANNA	Have you a resting-place reserved . . . or a family house in Bethlehem, perhaps?
ASA	Oh no! Nothing like that . . . but we are expecting to find something special here.
OTHERS IN ASA'S GROUP	Sh! Asa! Shh!
SARA	(*to her own family*) We said we should not tell.
ZADOK	We said it might not be wise.
REBEKAH	(*to the other family*) We are expecting to find an inn where we can rest before we register our names tomorrow. That is what we are expecting to find.
OLD MAN	We are all hoping to find rooms, my children. But I fear that we may be unlucky, for it is very late and others have come before us.
	(*Enter* SIMON *and* JACOB.)
RUTH	Did the lights come from an inn, brothers?
SIMON	It seems so, but we got no answer.
ANNA	You didn't knock loudly enough. Did you call out?
JACOB	Well . . . no. It seemed so quiet . . .
ASA	Let's all call together. We are Davids, so if there are rooms, we can share them out. Come on!
ALL YOUNG TRAVELLERS	(*moving to side*) Ho there! (*banging on the ground*) Ho there!
ASA	Travellers without!
ALL YOUNG TRAVELLERS	(*very loudly*) Travellers without!
	(*Enter* INNKEEPER.)
INNKEEPER	(*angrily*) Hold your peace! Ugh! Young ones! I should have guessed. Hold your peace, and move away from my inn.

ALL YOUNG TRAVELLERS	Peace be unto you, Innkeeper!
INNKEEPER	Peace! You say peace! You have made enough noise to raise the dead! And you have raised the living from their beds. Be off with you!
OLD MAN	(*anxiously*) Forgive these young ones, Innkeeper. It is for my sake that they have raised you from your bed. We've travelled for many days and these old bones of mine are weary.
INNKEEPER	(*more kindly*) It's very late old man.
OLD MAN	I know it's late, but we've come for Caesar's registration. We were late in hearing the decree and we made all the haste we could.
INNKEEPER	Well, you can't register at this time of night.
OLD MAN	I know that, Innkeeper. But have you some rooms where we can rest until daybreak?
INNKEEPER	Rooms! There are no rooms in my inn or in any house in Bethlehem. There is no room anywhere.
SIMON	We have some money.
JACOB	We can pay you well.
INNKEEPER	Why don't you young ones listen? I have told you . . . THERE IS NO ROOM. (*to Old Man*) I'm sorry, old man. You must do the best you can.
RUTH	We beg you . . . Find us a place somewhere.
ANNA	Just anywhere . . . Have you a stable?
INNKEEPER	(*firmly*) A stable! Not my stable! Of all places, not there!
SIMON	We only want a roof, and somewhere to lie down.
JACOB	Give us a bed of straw.

50

INNKEEPER	(*incredulously*) 'Give us a bed of straw!' Those are the words THEY said. (*putting hand to head in amazement*) A STABLE AND A BED OF STRAW!
ASA	What is it, Innkeeper?
INNKEEPER	(*shaking head*) Maybe my wife is right . . . Maybe this is a special night . . . Maybe . . .
ASA	Why do you talk of this being a special night? Is there some meaning in your words?
INNKEEPER	My wife thinks . . . We both think . . . I'll call her in. (*He goes to the side.*) Wife! Wife! Come out here!

(*Enter* INNKEEPER'S WIFE.)

WIFE	What is it husband?
INNKEEPER	These travellers . . . They asked for A STABLE AND A BED OF STRAW!
WIFE	(*putting hand on husband's arm*) Husband! I said that this was a special night.
OLD MAN	(*to Asa*) You spoke of something special yourself, Asa, when you first came into Bethlehem. You said that you were expecting to FIND SOMETHING SPECIAL here. What did you mean? We are all Davids, so tell us.
ASA	We will tell you. But first we must know if there has been a birth.
INNKEEPER, WIFE	(*unbelievingly*) BIRTH!
WIFE	But you were not here in Bethlehem, when the child was born.
INNKEEPER	How can you know about the birth?
ASA	(*smiling*) So there has been a birth?
SARA	Tell us . . . please . . . Was the child born to poor people, such as we are ourselves?

ZADOK	Was he born in a poor place, such as a stable?
REBEKAH	And was his cradle-bed, a manger?
INNKEEPER	(*backing away*) How can you know?
WIFE	You were not here.
OLD MAN	Asa! How can your family know of what happened here before you came to Bethlehem?
ASA	Some of this is written in the prophet's Great Book. Some we heard from the shepherds, on our way here.
INNKEEPER	(*turning to Wife*) So be it . . . We will tell the rest.

(*All gather round Innkeeper and Wife.*)

Early last evening, one of your kinsmen, Joseph of Nazareth, came to my inn. We had no rooms left, but . . .

WIFE	. . . But I said that Joseph and his wife must stay with us because she was with child and her time had come.
INNKEEPER	Joseph said, 'Just anywhere . . . a stable . . . give us a bed of straw.' That was all they asked.
WIFE	We made the stable ready and very soon the child, a boy, was born. The mother, Mary, wrapped the child in her own clothing and ever since . . . ever since . . .
INNKEEPER	. . . Ever since there has been a blessed calm . . . a peace . . . about this place.
OLD MAN	Was that why you wanted to send us all away?
WIFE	Yes . . . we wanted to keep the calm and peace.
ASA	There is a special feeling here. (*to others*) Can you feel it too?

(*All agree.*)

SARA	(*to Innnkeeper's Wife*) Can we see the child?

WIFE	Perhaps . . . a little later. After the birth, mother and child slept peacefully. So . . . perhaps . . .
ZADOK	We have come so far. Let us see the child.
REBEKAH	There will be many more to see him. Let us see him first.
INNKEEPER	Many more? Will there be others? Who will they be?
WIFE	Who will the others be?
ASA	Good people! All the world . . . in time, will come to Bethlehem. Listen! The shepherds will come first. We will tell you of it . . . There were shepherds, abiding in the fields, keeping watch over their flocks by night.
SARA	They saw an angel in the sky.
ZADOK	At first they were afraid.
REBEKAH	But the angel told them not to be afraid, saying, 'I bring you tidings of great joy, WHICH SHALL BE TO ALL MANKIND.' That is the important part. The news was for the whole world, for all of us.
INNKEEPER	What else did the angel say?
WIFE	What was this news?
ASA	The angel said, 'Unto you is born this day in the city of David, a Saviour, which is Christ the Lord'.
SARA	The angel said there would be a sign.
ZADOK	So that all the world should know the child.
REBEKAH	The angel said, 'Ye shall find the babe wrapped in swaddling clothes, lying in a manger.'
INNKEEPER	And this has happened here, in Bethlehem . . .
WIFE	In our stable!

INNKEEPER, WIFE GLORY TO GOD IN THE HIGHEST.

ALL PEACE, GOODWILL TOWARDS MEN.

(During the singing of 'The Virgin Mary had a baby boy' JOSEPH *and* MARY, *with the baby, come in and take up positions in centre. All characters already in arena raise arms in wonder, then put hands together in attitudes of prayer. They take up positions at side, looking at the baby.)*

The Virgin Mary had a baby boy,
The Virgin Mary had a baby boy,
The Virgin Mary had a baby boy,
And they say that his name was Jesus.
He come from the glory –
He come from the glorious kingdom;
He come from the glory –
He come from the glorious kingdom;
Oh yes! believer.
Oh yes! believer.
He come from the glory –
He come from the glorious kingdom.

(During the singing of 'Rise up, shepherd' the SHEPHERDS *enter. They bow to the baby, then take up suitable positions, some kneeling and all looking at the child.)*

1 There's a star in the East on Christmas morn;
  Rise up, shepherd, and follow;
  It will lead to the place where the Saviour's born;
  Rise up, shepherd, and follow.

  Chorus
  Rise up, shepherd, rise up, shepherd, and follow;
  Oh follow the star of Bethlehem, rise up, shepherd, and follow.

2 Leave your sheep, leave your sheep and leave your lambs;
  Rise up, shepherd, and follow;
  Leave your sheep, leave your sheep, leave your ewes and rams;
  Rise up, shepherd, and follow.

3 If you take good heed to the angel's words;
  Rise up, shepherd, and follow;
  You'll forget all your flocks, you'll forget your herds;
  Rise up, shepherd, and follow.

(*During the singing of 'Kings of Orient' the three* KINGS *come in.
They bow deeply to the baby, offer gifts during appropriate verse, then
take up positions, looking at the child.*)

The three kings

1 We three kings of Orient are;
  Bearing gifts we traverse afar
  Field and fountain, moor and mountain,
  Following yonder star:

Chorus

O star of wonder, star of night,
Star of royal beauty bright,
Westward leading still proceeding,
Guide us to they perfect light.

Melchior

2 Born a king on Bethlehem plain,
  Gold I bring to crown him again –
  King for ever, ceasing never,
  Over us all to reign:

Gaspar

3 Frankincense to offer have I;
  Incense owns a deity nigh:
  Prayer and praising, all men raising,
  Worship him, God most high:

Balthasar

4 Myrrh is mine; its bitter perfume
  Breathes a life of gathering gloom;
  Sorrowing, sighing, bleeding, dying,
  Sealed in the stone-cold tomb:

All

5 Glorious now, behold him arise,
   King and God, and sacrifice!
   Heaven sings alleluya,
   Alleluya the earth replies:

(*During the singing of 'What can I give him?' the boy* DAVID *comes in and kneels before the child, with Joseph's hand on his shoulder.*)

What can I give him,
   Poor as I am?
If I were a shepherd
   I would bring a lamb;
If I were a wise man
   I would do my part;
Yet what can I give him –
   Give my heart.

(*During the singing of the first verse of 'O little town of Bethlehem' the tableau remains still. Then the characters go out, during the singing of the other verses, headed by Joseph, Mary and the boy David.*)

1 O little town of Bethlehem,
   How still we see thee lie!
  Above thy deep and dreamless sleep
   The silent stars go by.
  Yet in thy dark streets shineth
   The everlasting light;
  The hopes and fears of all the years
   Are met in thee tonight.

2 O morning stars together
   Proclaim the holy birth,
And praises sing to God the King,
   And peace to men on earth;
For Christ is born of Mary;
   And, gathered all above,
While mortals sleep, the angels keep
   Their watch of wondering love.

3 How silently, how silently,
   The wondrous gift is given!
So God imparts to human hearts
   The blessings of his heaven.
No ear may hear his coming;
   But in this world of sin,
Where meek souls will receive him, still
   The dear Christ enters in.

4 O holy child of Bethlehem,
   Descend to us, we pray;
Cast out our sin, and enter in,
   Be born in us today.
We hear the Christmas Angels
   The great glad tidings tell:
O come to us, abide with us,
   Our Lord Emmanuel.

Music for the carols

Accompaniments can be found in *The Oxford Book of Carols*, *Faith, Folk and Nativity* (Galliard) and, for 'Kum ba yah', *Someone's singing, Lord* (A & C Black).

No room in the inn

In the bleak mid - winter *and* What can I give him?

Oh who would be a shepherd boy?

Three kings are here

Kings of Orient

Chorus

Song of the Nativity

Verses 1 and 3

Verses 2, 4 and 5

Standing in the rain

The Virgin Mary had a baby boy

Rise up, shepherd

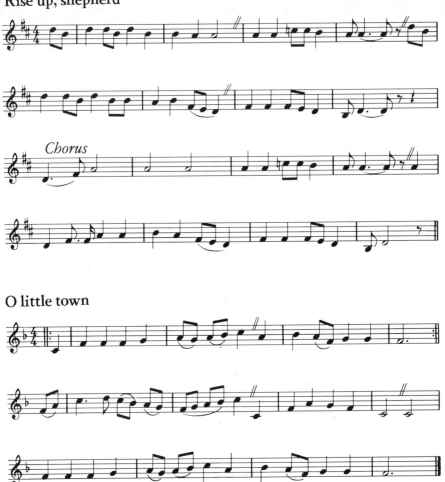

O little town

Kum ba yah

1 Kum ba yah, my Lord, kum ba yah,
Kum ba yah, my Lord, kum ba yah,
Kum ba yah, my Lord, kum ba yah,
  O Lord, kum ba yah.

2 Someone's singing, Lord, kum ba yah

3 Someone's praying, Lord, kum ba yah

4 Someone's hungry, Lord, kum ba yah

5 Someone's suffering, Lord, kum ba yah

6 Someone's lonely, Lord, kum ba yah

'Kum ba yah' means 'come by here' or 'be with us'.